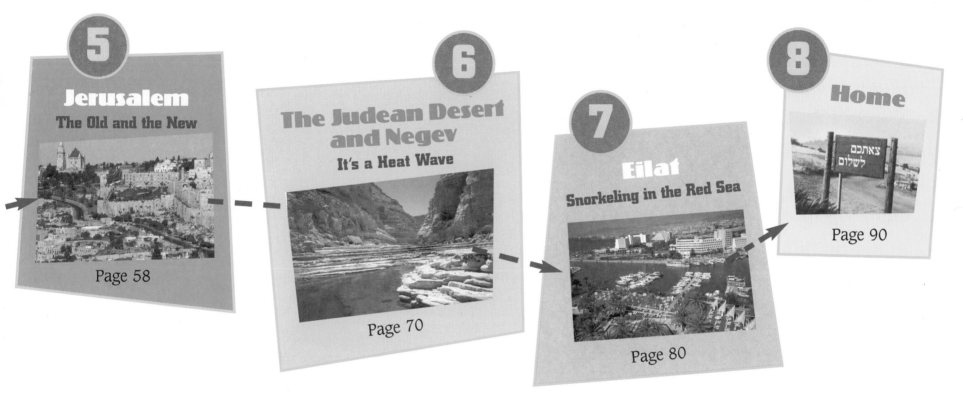

5 Jerusalem The Old and the New — Page 58

6 The Judean Desert and Negev It's a Heat Wave — Page 70

7 Eilat Snorkeling in the Red Sea — Page 80

8 Home — Page 90

Library of Congress Cataloging-in-Publication Data

Blumenthal, Scott

   The great Israel scavenger hunt / by Scott Blumenthal.

      p.cm.

   Summary: A vist to Israel by Daniel and his parents, a Jewish family, is guided by a scavenger hunt.

   Contents: Higher than the clouds — Haifa: the beautiful coast — The Galilee: rolling through the North — Tel Aviv: the city that never sleeps — Jerusalem: the old and the new — The Judean Desert and Negev: it's a heat wave — Eilat: snorkeling in the Red Sea — Home.

ISBN-10: 0-87441-711-2
ISBN-13: 978-0-87441-711-1

   1. Israel—Description and travel—Juvenile literature. [1. Israel—Description and travel.] I. Title.

DS107.5.B63 2003
915.69404'54—dc21

                                        2002043484

The publisher gratefully acknowledges the cooperation of the following sources of photographs: **Creative Image Photography** 94; **El Al Airlines** table of contents (1), 4–5, 6; **Gila Gevirtz** cover (Carmelit, Habimah Theater, cacti), table of contents (8), 17, 23, 26, 30, 39 (top), 46, 48, 49, 51 (left), 56 (left), 60, 61, 63, 74 (bottom), 76 (top), 82, 90–91; **Hanan Isachar** 52; **Israeli Scouts** 41; **Israel Ministry of Tourism** cover (Knesset), table of contents (2, 4, 5)18–19, 20, 28, 44–45, 51 (right), 56 (right), 58–59, 62, 67, 68, 73, 84, 85, 88; **Itamar Grinberg/ Israel Ministry of Tourism** cover (water park, Eilat port), table of contents (3, 6, 7) 9, 32–33, 35, 36, 39 (bottom), 42, 70–71, 72, 78, 80–81; **Tsur Pelly** 74, 75; **Hara Person** 27, 64, 76 (bottom); **Zionist Archives and Library** 22, 54

George Ulrich, illustrator: cover and pages 1, 2, 6, 12, 16, 20, 21, 37, 38, 47, 66, 77, 78, 85, 86, 94, 96

W9-AXW-671

El Al Israel Airlines is the
national airline of Israel.

The *Great* Israel Scavenger Hunt

Scott E. Blumenthal

Behrman House, Inc.

Contents

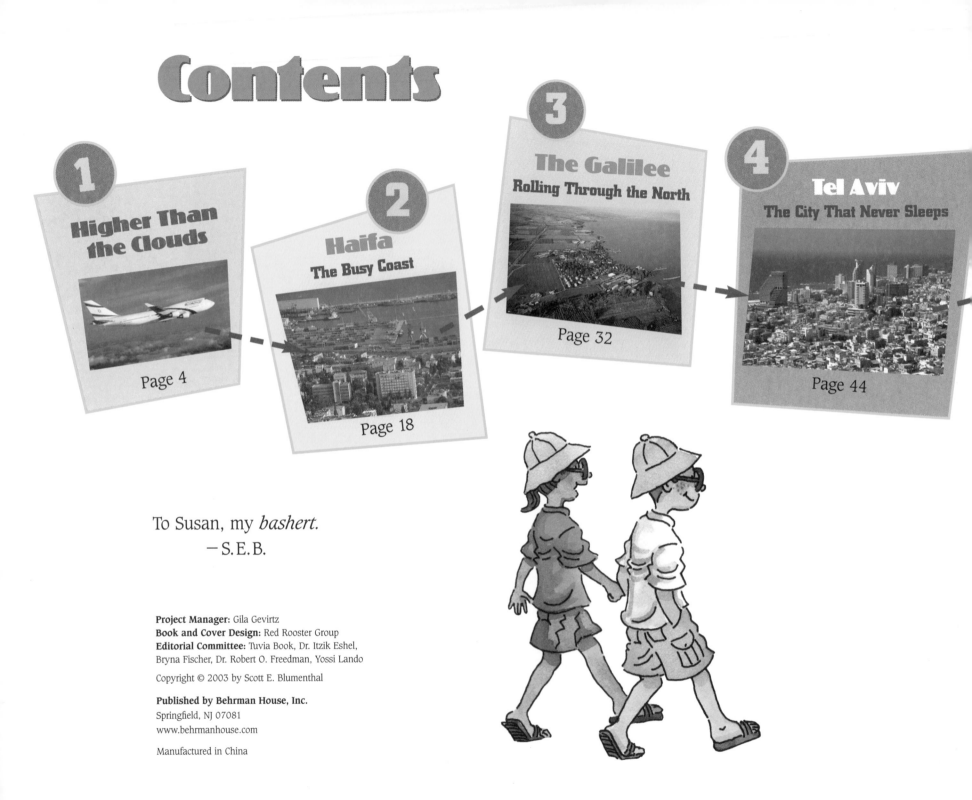

To Susan, my *bashert.*
— S.E.B.

Project Manager: Gila Gevirtz
Book and Cover Design: Red Rooster Group
Editorial Committee: Tuvia Book, Dr. Itzik Eshel, Bryna Fischer, Dr. Robert O. Freedman, Yossi Lando

Published by Behrman House, Inc.
Springfield, NJ 07081
www.behrmanhouse.com

Manufactured in China

Higher Than the Clouds

Daniel read the message across the envelope again:
Open only when you are higher than the clouds.
But from the window of the huge El Al jet, the
clouds seemed *very* high. "We're about to take
off," Daniel's father said, triple-checking his
backpack for their hats and suntan lotion.
"In about twelve hours we'll be in the Land
of Israel—*Eretz Yisrael*."

This lunch is served by El Al. Which of the foods do you like to eat? What do you think is inside the packets with the Hebrew writing?

"It will be like coming home again," said Daniel's mother. The jet's engines began to whir.

"How can it be like coming home again?" asked Daniel. "I've never been there!"

"Almost four thousand years ago," said Daniel's mother, "God promised Israel to Abraham, the first Jew. The Torah tells us that God said, 'All the land that you see, I will give to you, your children, and your children's children forever.' Ever since then, Jewish people have lived in Israel. So in a way, it *is* like coming home again."

Imagine Israel

What do you imagine Israel to be like?

In the spaces below, write a few words that you think will describe Israel.

Here's a start: Now you:

ancient   holy   _____   _____

Jewish   fun   _____   _____

After your trip, you can look back at this list and add more words. You may even want to change some!

ISRAEL IS THE HOME OF THE JEWISH PEOPLE

There are about 14,500,000 Jews in the world. About 5,000,000 live in Israel. The rest live in other countries, such as the United States, Canada, Italy, Mexico, Greece, and Australia.

Have you ever lived in another country? Do you know someone who has? Where?

_____

Sadly, Jews have not been treated well in some countries—for example, Ethiopia, Russia, and Syria. They have not been allowed to celebrate Jewish holidays, pray, or study Torah. Sometimes they have not been allowed to live or work where they wanted to. But because Israel is a Jewish country, many of these people could move there and live in safety.

Many other Jews moved to Israel from countries in which Jews lived in freedom. These Jews moved because they wanted to help build *Eretz Yisrael*. And, every year, many more Jews visit Israel because they love Israel and because it is the home of the Jewish people.

This Jewish family moved to Israel from Morocco, which is in Africa. They are eating traditional Moroccan foods.

"But Israel is really far away," Daniel said.

"Yes," said his mother. "More than six thousand miles away." She opened up a map of the world.

She drew a line from their home city, across the Atlantic Ocean, through Europe, then all the way to the far end of the Mediterranean Sea. "This part of the world is called the Middle East."

"And right here," Daniel's father said, pointing to a tiny piece of land, "is Israel." It was so small that the word *Israel* didn't even fit inside it.

How Far Away Is Israel?

Find where *you* live on this map (your teacher will help you) and draw a dot on it. Now, measure how far it is from where you live to Israel.

How many miles from Israel are *you*?

No matter how far away Israel is, it is always close to the hearts of the Jewish people.

KEY: 1 inch = 1,000 miles

How Big Is Israel?

Using the world map, color these countries as follows: **United States**, red; **Canada**, purple; **Russia**, green; **Syria**, yellow; **Israel**, blue.

Now, look at the size of Israel compared to these other countries.

Is Israel bigger or smaller than

the United States? _Smaller_

Canada? _Smaller_

Russia? _Smaller_

Syria? _Smaller_

In fact, Israel is one of the smallest countries in the world — but it is gigantic in the hearts of the Jewish people!

11

The jet raced down the runway and into the sky. Daniel and his parents held hands as they soared into the clouds.

Open only when you are higher than the clouds, Daniel read again. He looked out the window to make sure — yes, they were far above the clouds.

The envelope was from his grandfather. "*My* grandfather gave this to me when *I* first went to Israel," he had told Daniel at the airport. "And now," he continued, "I give it to *you* with a letter from me." Daniel opened the envelope.

Inside were several sheets of paper.

The first was a letter. It read:

Dear Daniel,

You are about to go on an exciting journey—the Great Israel Scavenger Hunt. As you travel through Israel, you will be a detective, searching for seven special objects. But on <u>this</u> scavenger hunt you don't take things. Instead, I have given you seven stickers, each with a picture of something to look for. I have also given you a map to put the stickers on as you find each object.

These are the rules for the Great Israel Scavenger Hunt:

1. As you travel, you will receive clues about what to look for next.

2. After you find each object, you will be asked to complete statements. When you do, you will discover a password. Then you can put the sticker for the object on the map. Each sticker belongs in only one place.

3. There will be one scavenger hunt object in each area you visit— never more.

All my love, Grandpa

P.S. You won't search alone. An important person will help you.

The State of ISRAEL

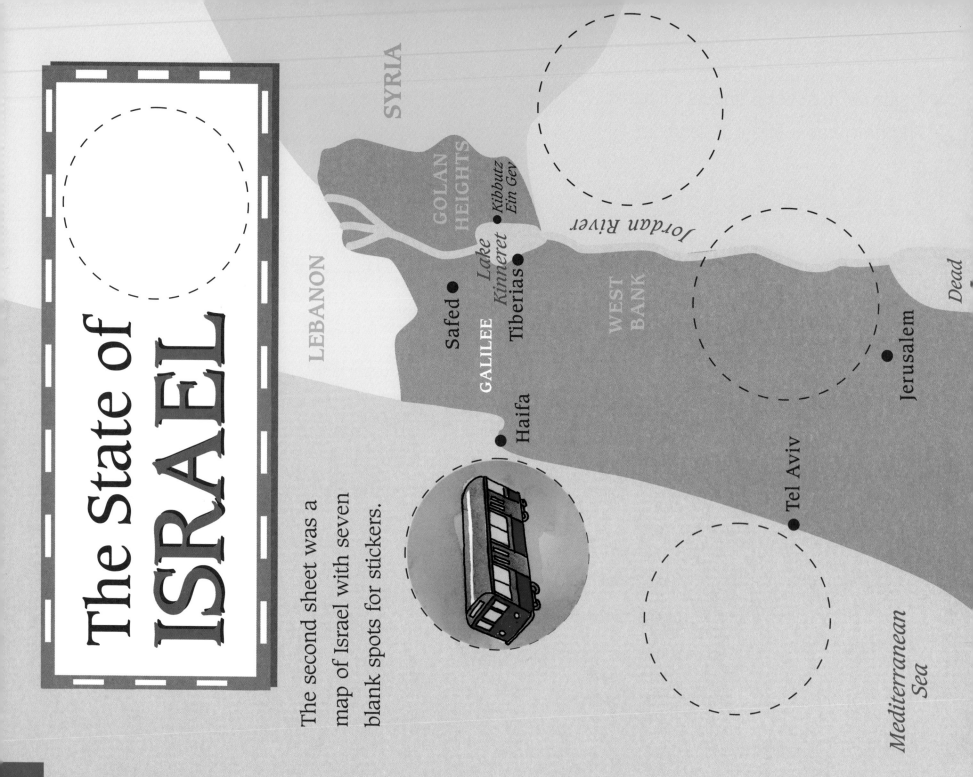

The second sheet was a map of Israel with seven blank spots for stickers.

SYRIA

LEBANON

GOLAN HEIGHTS

Safed

GALILEE

Lake Kinneret

Kibbutz Ein Gev

Tiberias

Haifa

Jordan River

WEST BANK

Jerusalem

Tel Aviv

Dead

Mediterranean Sea

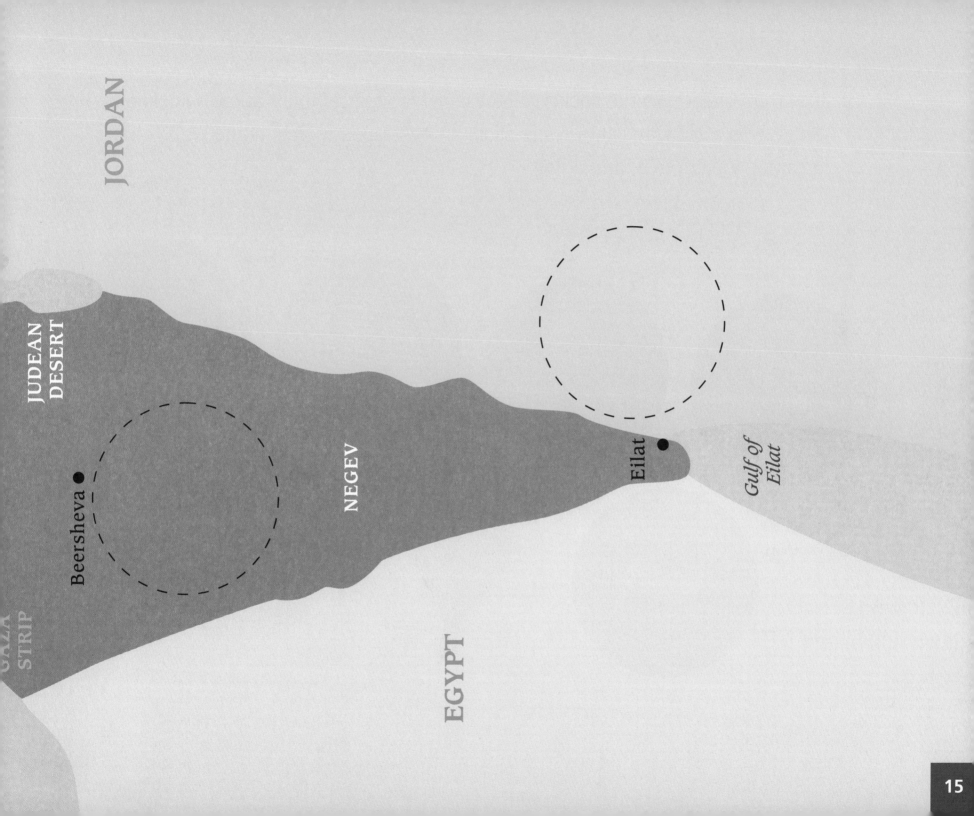

JORDAN

JUDEAN
DESERT

NEGEV

Beersheva

GAZA
STRIP

Eilat

Gulf of
Eilat

EGYPT

15

The third sheet was the sticker page. Daniel looked carefully at each sticker:
There was a subway car, a water slide, a skyscraper, a great stone wall,
a camel, a palm tree, and a flag.

The El Al jet dipped into the clouds and down toward Ben-Gurion Airport near Tel Aviv. Daniel was excited to be in Israel. He couldn't wait to begin the Great Israel Scavenger Hunt!

עזרה ראשונה
first aid

בית כנסת
synagogue

These signs are in Ben-Gurion Airport. What do you see that lets you know that you are in the home of the Jewish people?

Welcome to Israel ברוכים הבאים לישראל

You receive a big welcome —
B'ruchim Haba'im —
when you land at Ben-Gurion Airport.

Haifa is the third-largest city in Israel, after Jerusalem and Tel Aviv.

CHAPTER 2

Haifa

Haifa

The Busy Coast

"**S**halom," said Aunt Yael, greeting Daniel and his parents at Ben-Gurion Airport. Daniel was pleased. *Shalom* was the only Hebrew word he understood. He knew *shalom* means both "hello" and "goodbye," and that it also means "peace."

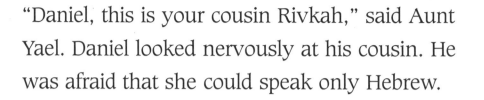

"Daniel, this is your cousin Rivkah," said Aunt Yael. Daniel looked nervously at his cousin. He was afraid that she could speak only Hebrew.

"Hi, Daniel," Rivkah said with a big smile. "We live down south, in Eilat, but we're going to see the whole country together. My mom will meet us back home. I'm going to be your tour guide! We're going to start in the city of Haifa."

Daniel's mother saw his surprise and said, "Almost everyone in Israel speaks Hebrew *and* English."

"Now *you* have to learn some Hebrew," said Rivkah. "I'll teach you."

How do we greet each other on Shabbat? **Hint:** One of the words is in this photo.

It's Not in the Torah!

For many years, Jews used Hebrew only for prayer and religious study. But about 120 years ago, Eliezer Ben-Yehuda—who lived in *Eretz Yisrael*—helped make Hebrew a modern, spoken language. He added words for inventions and ideas that didn't exist in the time of the Bible—words such as *car* and *electricity*. He created new Hebrew words from old ones and borrowed some words from other languages.

Today, Hebrew is the language of everyday life in Israel. It is still used for prayer and religious study. But it is also used for shopping, studying math, writing e-mails, and talking on cell phones.

See if you can match these Hebrew words with the pictures below:

טֶלֶוִיזְיָה   רַדְיוֹ   אָמֶרִיקָה   שׁוֹקוֹלָדָה   טֶלֶפוֹן

televizyah   *radyo*   *amerikah*   *shokoladah*   *telefon*

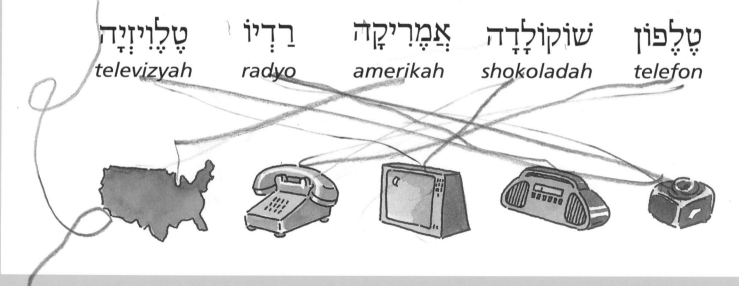

Eliezer Ben-Yehuda

Eliezer Ben-Yehuda and his wife, Deborah, published the first Hebrew newspaper in *Eretz Yisrael*.

Rivkah opened up a map of Israel to show Daniel where Haifa is. A note fell out. Rivkah read it, smiled, and said, "This must be a clue for the scavenger hunt!"

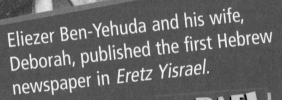

CLUE #1 — I help people move up and down and all around—but you'll find most of me underground.

"*You* know about the scavenger hunt?" asked Daniel in disbelief.

"*You* know about it, too?" asked Rivkah. Now it all made sense—Rivkah was the "important person" in Grandpa's letter. "Looks like we're in this together," she added. Now they were partners.

"We're driving north along the Mediterranean Sea, on the way to Haifa," said Rivkah. "Israel has loads of beaches and the swimming season is long—May through October."

חיפה
תל אביב
← 85
حيفا
تل ابيب
Haifa
Tel Aviv

This sign is written in the three main languages of Israel: **Hebrew, English**, and **Arabic**. Which Hebrew letters can you name? Which words are Arabic?

	Summer	Winter		Summer	Winter
Upper Galilee	95°	70°	**Jerusalem**	80°	50°
Haifa	85°	60°	**Beersheva**	85°	70°
Tel Aviv	85°	60°	**Eilat**	95°	70°

"There's Haifa!" called Rivkah. She pointed to a mountain with thousands of pine trees. "That's Mount Carmel." Daniel saw that there was a city along its slope, facing the sea. Haifa reminded Daniel of San Francisco, which also has views of the water and the city from its hilly streets.

They drove to Hadar Hacarmel, the business section of Haifa. "Hadar Hacarmel is always busy. It's filled with stores, restaurants, and movie theaters," said Rivkah. There was so much going on: the chatter of Hebrew, the music of a guitarist singing a rock-and-roll song (in Hebrew!), the spicy aroma of foods that Daniel did not recognize. All of it was mixed together in the warmth of the Israeli sunshine.

Munchies

Kids in Israel like to eat pizza and hamburgers, just like kids here. They also eat foods that are favorites in the Middle East. What will you have for lunch when you go to Israel?

Welcome to Falafel King!

Falafel — Ground chickpeas, fried

Ḥummus — A thick, creamy dip made from chickpeas

Israeli Salad — A mixture of fresh veggies, including diced tomatoes and cucumbers

Teḥina — A tasty sesame dip

Everything above is served in a pita — a fresh, warm, flat bread with a pocket.

See if you can find all the foods hidden inside the pita:

☑ Falafel ☑ Pizza
☑ Salad ☑ Teḥina
☑ Ḥummus ☑ Pita

Hint: *The words may appear across, backwards, or down.*

A	T	I	P	S	D	L
B	W	J	I	C	F	A
H	D	R	Z	H	E	T
C	E	M	Z	R	F	A
F	A	L	A	F	E	L
A	A	N	I	H	E	T
S	A	L	A	D	S	N
S	U	M	M	U	H	M

Let's Eat Out in Israel!

MAC DAVID
MAC DAVID

מק דויד
מק דויד

An Israeli restaurant with an American flavor!

Israel is filled with kosher restaurants. It also has kosher juice bars. Where are the clues that tell you this is a kosher juice bar? Hint: One clue is in Hebrew. The other is in English.

"Falafel! Ḥummus!" called out a nearby shop owner. That sounded *good*—everyone was ready for lunch!

When they entered the restaurant, a security guard searched their backpacks. "It's to make sure that everyone is safe," said Rivkah. "When I finish high school, I'm going to join the Israeli army," she said proudly. "Then *I'll* help protect everyone."

After lunch, they went for a ride on Haifa's famous cable car, a see-through glass bubble soaring high above the city. The sea sparkled in the distance. Daniel saw that the beach wrapped around Mount Carmel in a giant half-circle, forming a harbor. "Haifa's port is the biggest in Israel," said Rivkah. "Ships sail in and out all the time. See?"

Like many other Israelis, these children will join the Israeli Defense Force (IDF) when they are 18 years old. Girls serve two years in the IDF and boys serve three years.

When you visit Haifa you can go on the cable car ride.

Daniel saw little sailboats, giant ocean liners, and freighters. One freighter was being loaded with large crates. "Products that are made or grown in Israel are sent to places all over the world," said Rivkah. "Computer chips, candy, clothing, and lots of fruits and vegetables!"

Time to *ship off!*

Find some of the products that are shipped from Haifa by unscrambling the word on each crate.

cilotghn — clothing

caynd — candy

oarnegs — oranges

ejweylr — Jewelery

tsoomate — tomatoes

fslorwe — flowers

Many Jews living outside of Israel try to buy products that were made there. For example, they buy food, bathing suits, jewelry, seder plates, and Kiddush cups that were made in Israel. Why do you think they do that?

_____

_____

The last stop on the Carmelit is called The Mother's Park, **Gan Ha'eim**.

After the cable car ride, Rivkah said, "I've got a great idea. Let's take the subway."

"Subway? No way! There's no subway in Israel," said Daniel in disbelief.

"There sure is, and it's called the Carmelit. The Carmelit goes up and down Mount Carmel. It starts at the port level, then goes up to Hadar Hacarmel, then up to Carmel Center, and then back down again," Rivkah insisted.

"That's it!" said Daniel. "'I help people move up and down and all around...'"

"'...But you'll find most of me underground!'" said Rivkah. They gave each other a high-five. They had found their first scavenger hunt puzzle piece.

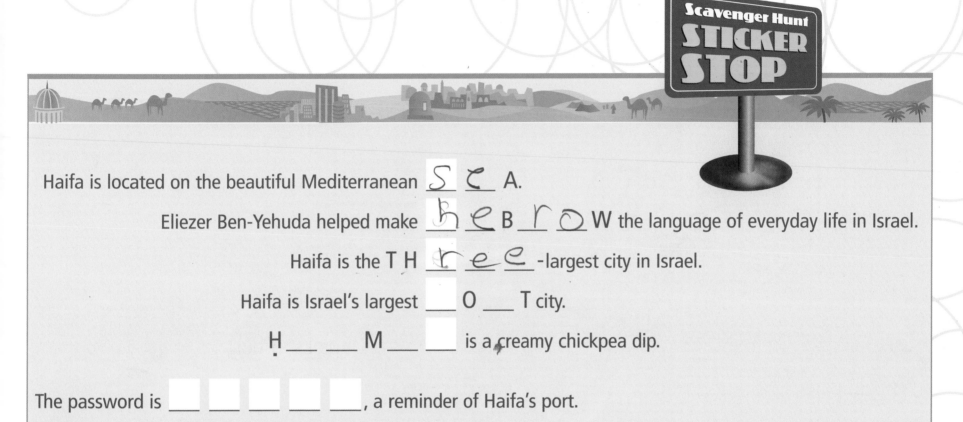

Haifa is located on the beautiful Mediterranean S E A.

Eliezer Ben-Yehuda helped make H e B r o W the language of everyday life in Israel.

Haifa is the T H r e e -largest city in Israel.

Haifa is Israel's largest ___ O ___ T city.

H. ___ ___ M ___ ___ is a creamy chickpea dip.

The password is ___ ___ ___ ___ ___, a reminder of Haifa's port.

➤ **When your teacher says it's okay, turn to the map of Israel on pages 14–15 and place your Haifa sticker in its spot!**

The Upper Galilee is
the rainy part of Israel.

CHAPTER 3

Israel **LOCATOR**

Golani Junction

The Galilee

Rolling Through the North

Looking out the car window, Daniel noticed that the land seemed *very* green. All around were rolling hills and grassy fields, spotted with silver-and-green olive trees. "We're in northern Israel," said Rivkah. "It's called the Galilee—or *Galil* in Hebrew.

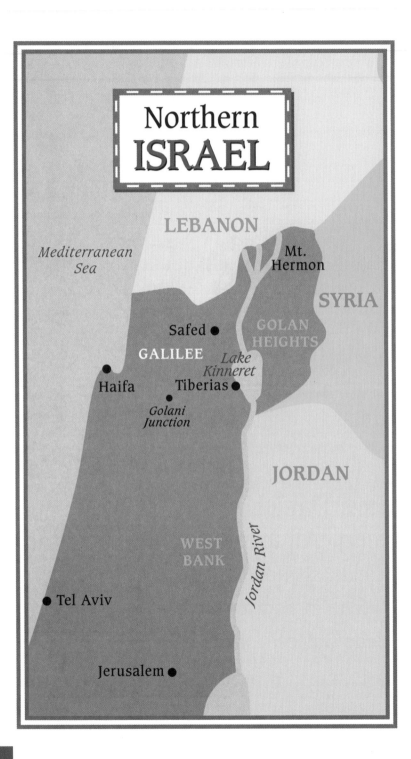

Northern ISRAEL

LEBANON

Mediterranean Sea

Mt. Hermon

SYRIA

Safed

GOLAN HEIGHTS

GALILEE

Lake Kinneret

Haifa

Tiberias

Golani Junction

JORDAN

Jordan River

WEST BANK

Tel Aviv

Jerusalem

Daniel took a pair of sunglasses from his backpack. Taped to it was a note—another clue:

CLUE#2 To find a park with super slides, check out where the water hides.

Everywhere Daniel and Rivkah went in the Galilee, they searched for the slides.

They searched at Golani Junction, where forests of evergreen trees towered above. "It's a mitzvah to plant trees," said Rivkah. "Trees give us shade and all kinds of fruit. Orange, pear, date, lemon, and grapefruit trees grow in Israel."

Plant a Tree of Your Own

God made every tree grow that is beautiful to see and that gives food (Genesis 2:9).

The Torah teaches us that trees are important. It even has laws against cutting them down!

For more than one hundred years, the Jewish National Fund, or JNF, has helped build the Land of Israel by planting trees. In fact, it has planted more than 200 million of them! With the help of the JNF, you can plant a tree. It is a Jewish custom to plant trees in honor of someone, maybe a parent or teacher, or in memory of someone who has died.

In whose honor would *you* like to plant a tree?

My great Grampa named grampa Danny

Israeli children plant trees on **Tu B'Shevat**, the New Year of the Trees.

Fun Fact

Lake Kinneret takes its name from the Hebrew word *kinor*. *Kinor* meant "harp" in ancient times. Lake Kinneret is shaped like a harp.

They searched at the Sea of Galilee—also called Lake Kinneret. "Lake Kinneret is the only freshwater lake in Israel. One-third of our drinking water comes from there," Rivkah explained.

They searched the Tiberias Hot Springs, pools of hot mineral water created by an underground spring. "In ancient times," said Rivkah, "people thought that these waters could cure sickness."

"Or make you into a hard-boiled egg!" said Daniel, his toe barely touching the water.

The Tiberias Hot Springs bubble up from more than a mile underground. They reach a steamy 140 degrees!

Farther north, they searched in Safed. They walked through a part of the city called the Artists' Colony, where many painters, sculptors, and craftspeople work. "Every year, at Ḥanukkah, my family lights beautiful candles that are made here," said Rivkah.

You're the Artist!

Imagine that you are an artist from Safed. Use crayons or markers to color the candles any way you like.

They searched as they drove east. "This is the Golan Heights," said Rivkah. "Lots of Israelis come here for vacation. You can hike in the mountains, bird-watch, and visit the Banyas National Park."

High up in the Golan Heights, they searched the slopes of Mount Hermon, the tallest mountain in Israel. "The mountain is covered with wildflowers now," said Rivkah, "but in the wintertime you can ski here. You can soak in the Tiberias Hot Springs in the morning, then go skiing on Mount Hermon in the afternoon!"

Five hundred years ago, the greatest rabbis in Israel came to Safed to study and teach. Today, after you visit Safed, you can take software home to help you continue your studies.

An ancient fortress in the Golan Heights, covered in snow

A Day in the Life
of an Israeli Kid

As they drove through the Golan Heights,
Rivkah described her typical school day.

6 A.M.	Good morning! *Boker tov!* Time to get up. In Israel, kids go to school six days a week—every day except Shabbat.
8 A.M.	School starts. This year, we're learning English, Jewish history, math, and science. We also study music and art.
1 P.M.	School's out! I take the bus home and eat lunch. (My favorite is grilled cheese.)
2 P.M.	Homework time. When I'm done, I play with my friends or read.
4 P.M.	I go to Israeli Scouts—*Tzofim.* (It's like the Girl Scouts and Boy Scouts of America.)
6 P.M.	Dinner
7 P.M.	Relax with my family and watch TV or play games on the computer.
9 P.M.	Time for bed. Good night! *Lailah tov!*

Write a schedule of your typical school day on this chart. Compare it with Rivkah's. What is the same? What is different?

Time   Activity
_____   _____
             _____
_____   _____
             _____
_____   _____
             _____
_____   _____
             _____
_____   _____
             _____
_____   _____
             _____
_____   _____
             _____
_____   _____

The *Tzofim* welcomes all Israeli boys and girls—Jews and non-Jews—to become members.

As they drove back along the eastern shore of Lake Kinneret, they came to the Luna Gal Water Park. Rivkah and Daniel looked around in amazement. There were pedal boats, sailboards, kayaks, water parachutes, and...

"Water slides!" they cried out together.

Luna Gal is located near Kibbutz Ein Gev. It has lots of great ways to cool off on a hot day.

The northern part of Israel is called the ___ A ___ ___ L ___ E.

The T ___ B ___ ___ I ___ S Hot Springs feel like a hot tub.

Israel's giant freshwater lake is called Lake ___ I ___ N ___ R ___ T.

The artists of S ___ ___ ___ D make beautiful Ḥanukkah candles.

Mount H E R ___ ___ ___ is the tallest mountain in Israel.

The password is ___ ___ ___ ___ ___, a reminder of the rolling hills and valleys of the Galilee.

When your teacher says it's okay, turn to the map of Israel on pages 14–15 and place your Galilee sticker in its spot!

Tel Aviv is south of Haifa, along the coast of the Mediterranean Sea.

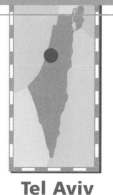

CHAPTER 4

Tel Aviv

Tel Aviv

The City That Never Sleeps

"Tel Aviv is called 'The City that Never Sleeps' because there's always so much going on," said Rivkah as she guided Daniel and his parents along busy King George Street. "Some stores are open until midnight. Some are even open all night!"

Since they had arrived in Tel Aviv, Daniel's eyes had been wide open with wonder. He had known about Israel's ancient and holy places, but *this* was a surprise—streets filled with cars, people hurrying to buses and taxis, and skyscrapers towering overhead.

"We have a lot of exploring to do," said Daniel's mother. "But first, how about some ice cream at Dizengoff Center?"

"Yes!" exclaimed Rivkah and Daniel. It was hot, and ice cream—*glidah*—sounded great.

As Daniel's mom handed Rivkah a double scoop of chocolate chocolate chip, Daniel saw that a note was wrapped around the cone. Another clue!

 **CLUE #3** Near the sands of Tel Aviv's shore, I climb and climb thirty-six floors.

"Hmm. That sounds exciting," said Daniel.

What flavor *glidah* do you like? Can you find the Hebrew word for "ice cream" in this picture?

Only in ISRAEL!

In many ways, Dizengoff Center is like your local shopping mall. It has video arcades, movie theaters, and, of course, ice cream shops. But it's also different. You won't see movie posters in Hebrew at your neighborhood shopping center!

Circle those things below that you might see only in malls in Israel.

FUN FACT

One out of every three Israelis—more than two million people—lives in or around Tel Aviv, and more than ninety-five percent of the people in Tel Aviv are Jewish!

"Tel Aviv is exciting!" said Rivkah as they walked along King George Street. "Jewish people built Tel Aviv about one hundred years ago. Before then, there was nothing here except sand. *Now* look at it! There's so much to do and see. Let's start exploring."

סכנה !
כאן בונים
DANGER !
CONSTRUCTION AREA

Everywhere you go in Israel you see new buildings being built and signs like this saying: *"Sakanah! Kan bonim."*

When they reached Habimah Square, Rivkah explained, "This is Habimah, the first theater in Israel. Habimah puts on plays only in Hebrew. But don't worry—there are headphones for people who want to hear the play in English!

"Headphones are just the beginning of technology in Tel Aviv," Rivkah continued. "Some of Israel's most creative scientists work and teach at Tel Aviv University. They are always inventing something new. I heard they are making robots that can speak Hebrew."

Computers & **Science**

Israel is a world leader in science—and computers, too. It makes and sells computer parts and software to countries all around the world. Half the homes in Israel have a computer in them.

Imagine you are building a robot of your own. What would you call your robot? _____

List two ways your robot would help people.

1. _____

2. _____

You already have learned several Hebrew words and expressions. If you could teach your robot to speak Hebrew, which words would you want to teach it? Why? _____

_____

As they walked south, Rivkah pointed ahead and said, "There's Tel Aviv's outdoor market, *Shuk Hacarmel*. You can buy almost anything at the *shuk*—sunglasses, stuffed animals, video games."

In Israel, you're never too young to start learning about **hamahsheiv**—the computer.

There are open-air markets in cities and villages all over Israel.

Daniel's eyes lit up when they arrived at the *shuk*. He spied a blue Israeli sun hat, or *kova tembel,* tried it on, and checked himself out in a mirror. Pleased with what he saw, he bought the hat. Then they continued on their way south.

"Rivkah," said Daniel, suddenly stopping, his eyes looking up, up, up. Look! I found it—for the scavenger hunt! Wow—this building is even taller than the one my mother works in."

"This is the Shalom Tower," said Rivkah. "It was built in 1964, the first skyscraper in Israel!"

The Shalom Tower is special because it was Israel's first skyscraper. Today there are other skyscrapers, including Tel Aviv's Azrieli Center towers.

When you want ice cream in Israel, just ask for G ___ ___ D ___ ___ [ ] .

Tel Aviv's nickname is "The City that Never ___ L ___ ___ P ___ [ ] ."

Skyscrapers are tall [ ] ___ ___ I ___ ___ I ___ G ___ .

One of Tel Aviv's busiest streets is King ___ ___ O [ ] ___ ___ E Street.

___ ___ Z ___ N G ___ ___ ___ [ ] Center is a shopping mall — Israeli style.

Israel is the home of the ___ E [ ] ___ ___ ___ H people.

The password is [ ][ ][ ][ ][ ][ ] ___ ___ ___ ___ ___ ___ , a reminder of the language of our people and of all Israel.

➤ **When your teacher says it's okay, turn to the map of Israel on pages 14–15 and place your Tel Aviv sticker in its spot!**

Not far from the Shalom Tower they came to the Independence Hall Museum. "This is where David Ben-Gurion, Israel's first prime minister, declared Israel's independence," explained Rivkah.

David Ben-Gurion

Today you can walk into the very room where Ben-Gurion made his famous speech in 1948. It looks exactly as it did on that day.

"What's a prime minister?" asked Daniel.

"The prime minister is the head of the Israeli government, just as the prime minister of Canada and the president of the United States are heads of their governments," answered Rivkah.

Daniel and Rivkah walked toward the shore. "Look, down there, that's the old section of Tel Aviv. It's called Jaffa. In fact, the full name of the city is Tel Aviv-Jaffa," Rivkah continued.

"Jaffa's mentioned in the Bible—it's the city that Jonah sailed from before he was swallowed by the big fish. Many artists live there now."

That evening, Daniel and Rivkah were so tired they could hardly say good night. "Tel Aviv may be the city that never sleeps," Daniel said, "but I sure do." And off he went to dream of tomorrow's adventure.

You Be the Tour Guide!

Now that you're practically an expert on the city, help plan a tour of Tel Aviv for your family. Bring them to four different places, beginning with the Shalom Tower. Draw a line from one place to the next to show the path you will take!

In the space below, write the name of each location and list one fact about it.

1. <u>Shalom Tower: the first</u> <u>skyscraper built in Israel</u>

2. _____

   _____

3. _____

   _____

4. _____

   _____

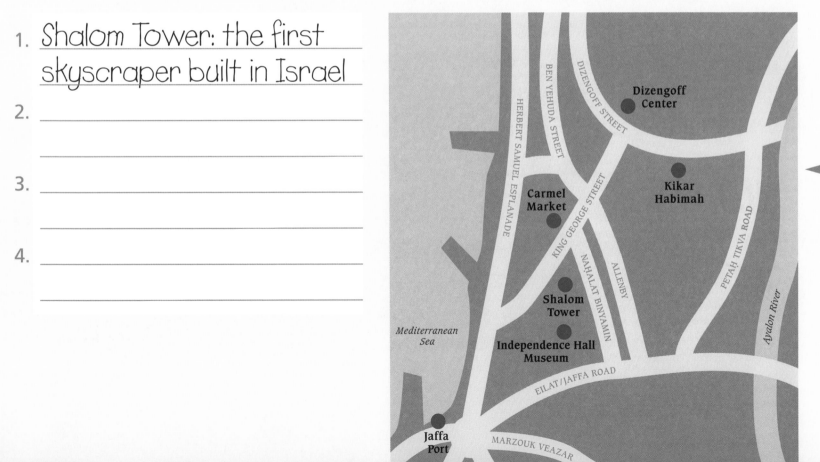

Jaffa The Oldest Port in the World

Jaffa is next door to Tel Aviv. It is more than 4,000 years old and may be the oldest port in the world!

לנמל
TO THE PORT →

When you go to Jaffa, be sure to go *l'namal,* to the port!

Send a Postcard Home

You've already learned a lot about Israel. Write a postcard to a friend describing two of your favorite places in *Eretz Yisrael!*

Dear

Shalom

Jerusalem is built on several mountains. This one is Mount Zion.

CHAPTER 5

Israel **LOCATOR**

Jerusalem

Jerusalem

The Old and the New

Through the window of the bus, Daniel saw that most of the buildings in Jerusalem were made of a stone that looks almost golden in daylight. It is called Jerusalem stone.

"Like Tel Aviv-Jaffa, Jerusalem is two cities in one," Rivkah explained. "We're in the New City. It's filled with apartment buildings, supermarkets, movie theaters, and lots of traffic. Later we'll go to the Old City. You'll feel as if you've gone back in time!"

Jerusalem is sometimes called "The City of Gold."

In Liberty Bell Park in Jerusalem, there is a roller-skating rink and a model of Philadelphia's Liberty Bell.

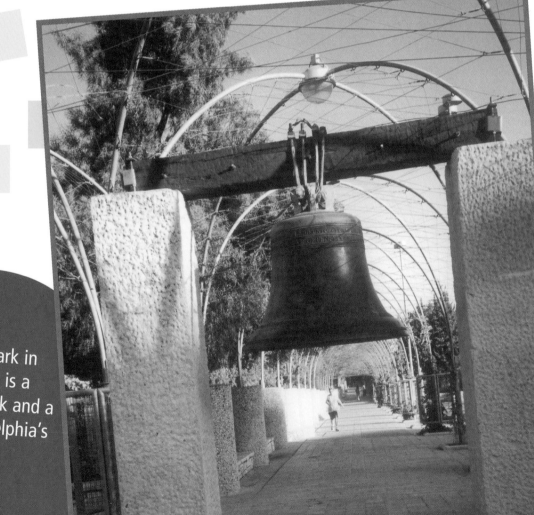

The bus stopped at the building where the Knesset—the elected leaders of Israel—make decisions about how to run the country. "Great!" said Daniel's mother as she read *The Jerusalem Post.* "The newspaper says that the Knesset is meeting today."

Just then, a note fell out from between the pages of the newspaper. "Our next clue!" Rivkah said.

 **CLUE #4** I've stood for more than two thousand years, and every day I hear your prayers.

If you want to read about what's going on in Israel, you can check out *The Jerusalem Post*, an all-English Israeli newspaper.

The building where the Knesset meets is also called the Knesset. Across the street from the Knesset is a fifteen-foot, seven-branched menorah!

This is Israel's state emblem. The menorah is an ancient Jewish symbol. The olive branches stand for Israel's yearning for peace.

As they went inside, Rivkah explained, "Jerusalem is Israel's capital—like Washington, D.C." They walked upstairs to a balcony where visitors can see and listen to Knesset meetings. They could hear the voices from the giant room below, but everyone was speaking in Hebrew.

"What are they saying?" whispered Daniel.

"They are talking about a new law to help keep the roads safe," Rivkah answered.

After they left the Knesset, Daniel, his parents, and Rivkah took a bus to the Old City of Jerusalem. They walked next to a gigantic stone wall, then passed under a great stone archway. "For Jewish people," said Rivkah, "Jerusalem—*Yerushalayim*—is the holiest city in the world."

"Why?" asked Daniel.

"King David made Jerusalem the capital of his kingdom more than 3,000 years ago. Then his son, King Solomon, built the Holy Temple—the *Beit Hamikdash*—here," answered Rivkah.

The winding cobblestone streets were too narrow to permit cars and buses to pass through. And all the buildings were made of Jerusalem stone. "Rivkah was right," Daniel said to his mom. "It's like we've gone back in time."

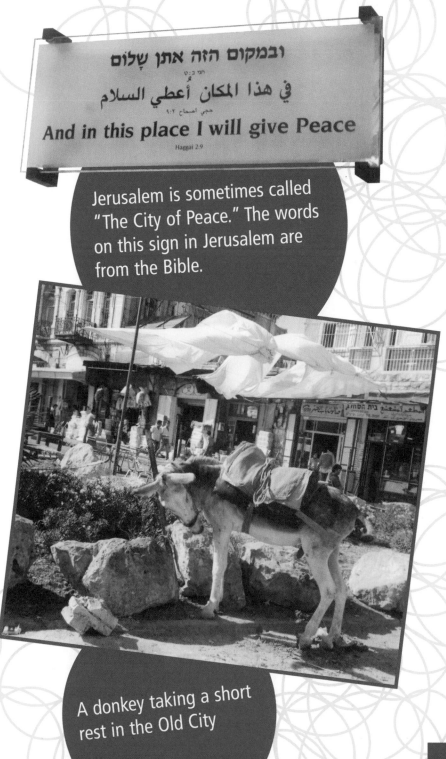

ובמקום הזה אתן שלום

في هذا المكان أعطي السلام

And in this place I will give Peace

Haggai 2:9

Jerusalem is sometimes called "The City of Peace." The words on this sign in Jerusalem are from the Bible.

A donkey taking a short rest in the Old City

Seeking Peace רוֹדֵף שָׁלוֹם

The mitzvah of seeking peace is called *rodef shalom*. *Rodef shalom* teaches us that we should do our best to live peacefully with others.

Make a list of five rules that will help your classroom be a place where people can seek peace. Here's a start:

1. Don't say mean things to one another.

2. _____

3. _____

4. _____

5. _____

There are many great places kids can visit around Jerusalem — parks, swimming pools, the Tisch Gardens Biblical Zoo, the Botanical Gardens, The Play Sculpture Garden at the Israel Museum, and Neot Kedumim Nature Reserve, where you can make your own pita!

Working for **Peace**

Israel is the homeland of the Jewish people, but many other religious groups also live there. More than one million Arabs live in Israel. Most practice the religion of Islam and are called Muslims. A smaller number of Arabs are Christians. Christians and Muslims also consider Jerusalem a holy city. Sadly, Christians, Muslims, and Jews have sometimes fought wars over who owns Jerusalem.

Think back to an argument you had with someone. Maybe you thought it was your turn to choose a game, or that a new toy or CD belonged to you, not to your brother or sister. What can you do to settle such disagreements without fighting?

_____

_____

Describe one thing people of different religions can do to get along when they disagree.

_____

_____

"I know it!" said Rivkah as they walked along Jewish Quarter Road. "The next scavenger hunt piece!"

"What is it?" Daniel asked.

"Three thousand years ago almost *every* Jew lived in the Land of Israel," Rivkah answered. "King David chose Mount Moriah, the highest and most beautiful spot in the city, on which to build the Holy Temple.

"Jews came from all over Israel to pray there. But about four hundred years later, the Temple was destroyed by the Babylonians. Most Jews were forced out of the land of Israel. When we were able to return, about sixty years later, we built the Second Temple. But it was destroyed by the Romans about six hundred years later. Only one wall was left standing."

"For how long?" asked Daniel.

"Almost two thousand years, and counting," said Rivkah, pointing ahead.

And there, in the distance, stood the most holy Jewish place in the world, the Western Wall—the *Kotel*.

The *Kotel* is part of a Second Temple supporting wall. Each stone is *very* large—one yard tall.

Many people come to pray at the **Kotel.** These people are participating in a bar mitzvah service.

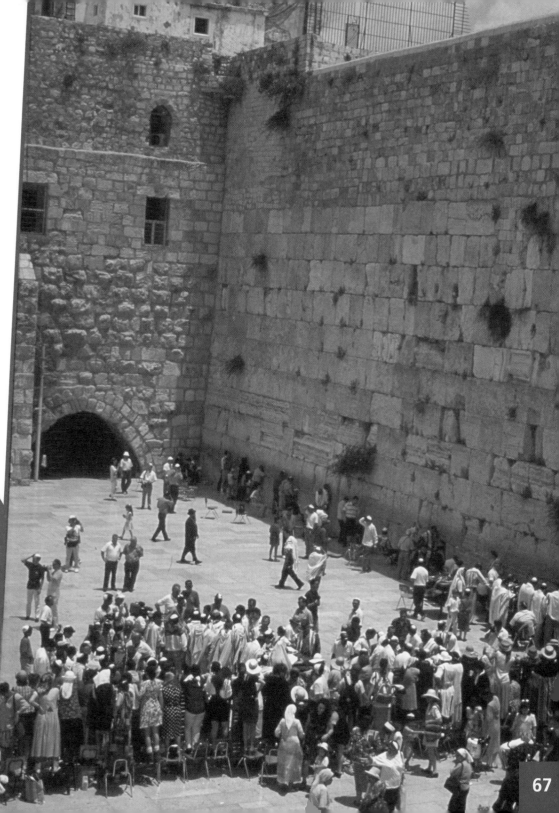

Write a Note to God

Prayer notes between the stones of the **Kotel**

Thousands of people have written prayers to God and put them between the stones of the *Kotel*.

Write your own prayer to God. For example, you might thank God for something good in your life, or ask God to help you become a more patient person. One day, when you are in Israel, you can visit the *Kotel* and place your prayer between the stones!

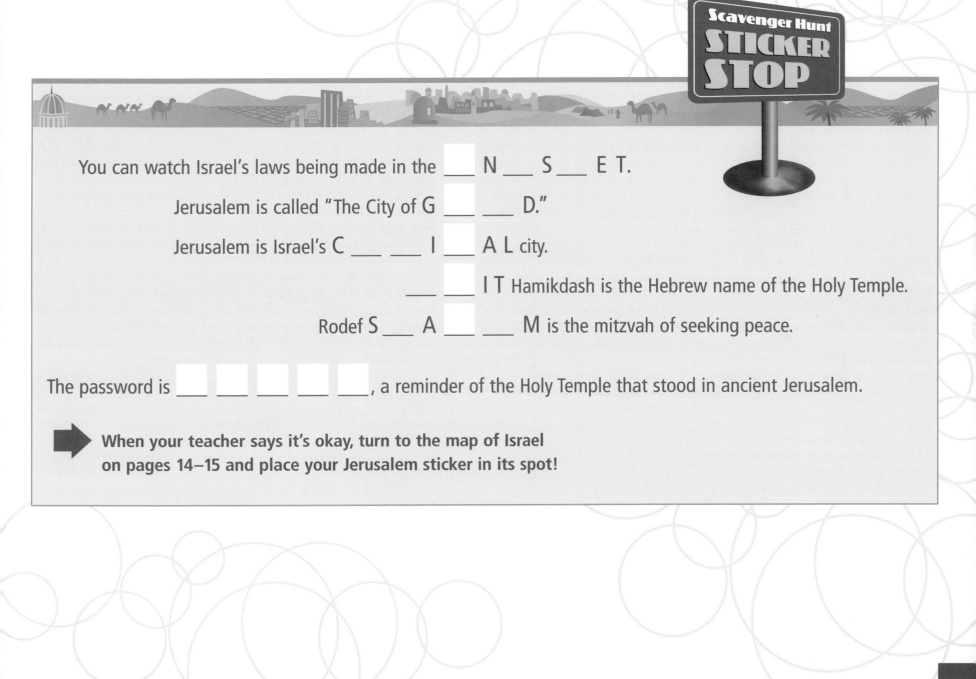

You can watch Israel's laws being made in the ___ N ___ S ___ E T.

Jerusalem is called "The City of G ___ ___ D."

Jerusalem is Israel's C ___ ___ I ___ A L city.

___ ___ I T Hamikdash is the Hebrew name of the Holy Temple.

Rodef S ___ A ___ ___ M is the mitzvah of seeking peace.

The password is ___ ___ ___ ___ ___ , a reminder of the Holy Temple that stood in ancient Jerusalem.

When your teacher says it's okay, turn to the map of Israel on pages 14–15 and place your Jerusalem sticker in its spot!

Ein Avdat National Park is in the middle of the Negev.

CHAPTER 6

The Judean Desert and Negev

Masada

It's a Heat Wave

"We're almost at the top. This is an ancient fortress called Masada, where our ancestors stood up against the Romans," said Rivkah, shining her flashlight along the winding Snake Trail. "And just in time. The sun is rising!"

Daniel saw rocky canyons and high cliffs that stretched out in all directions. Here in the south, Israel looked like a giant desert.

At Masada, archeologists have found the ancient remains of a synagogue, King Herod's northern palace, storerooms, and bakeries.

ISRAEL

Fun Fact

Archeologists are people who study how others lived long ago—what their homes, coins, clothing, and schools looked like. Ancient objects are buried all over Israel. Some have been buried for hundreds of years. Masada, Jerusalem, and Jaffa are some of the places where you can find them.

"Masada is in the Judean Desert," said Rivkah.

They drove on and Rivkah explained, "Next to Masada is the Dead Sea. The water there is so salty that it is called the Sea of Salt — *Yam Hamelaḥ* in Hebrew. The salt and minerals make the water *thick*. That makes it really easy to float but almost impossible to swim!"

When they arrived at the Dead Sea, Daniel and Rivkah put on their bathing suits. "Some people take Dead Sea mud baths because it's good for the skin," said Rivkah. "I think it's just fun to play in!"

Daniel and Rivkah covered themselves in the slimy black mud. They even painted their faces with it.

After showering, Daniel reached for his towel to dry off. As he opened it, a note flew into the air. He quickly caught it. It was the next clue.

CLUE #5 I'm called the "ship of the desert" though I haven't a sail— just a mountain-shaped hump 'tween my snout and my tail.

The Dead Sea is 1,300 feet below sea level—the *lowest* point on Earth. The mud baths may be the most *fun* place on Earth!

Looking at modern Beersheva, it may be hard to remember that our ancestors Abraham and Jacob once walked here.

Many different kinds of cacti grow in the Negev.

Daniel showed the note to Rivkah, who said, "This sounds like a live one. Come on, we'd better get going." And off they drove, heading southward to the Negev.

"The Negev is a huge desert. It's so big that it takes up almost half of Israel!" explained Rivkah as they got out of the car. "We're in Beersheva—the largest city in the Negev. Before the State of Israel was born in 1948, few people lived here, and there wasn't much water for drinking or growing food.

"Today, pipes carry water here all the way from Rosh Ha'ayin, which is northeast of Tel Aviv! Now the Negev has lots of great stuff—Ben-Gurion University, the Negev Museum, and—"

"Camel rides!" called a voice.

A Hopeful People

The unofficial national anthem of Israel is "Hatikvah," which means "The Hope." When the Second Temple was destroyed, our people were forced out of Israel. But we never lost hope that one day the land would be ours again. After almost two thousand years of waiting and working together for an independent Jewish state, our dream came true in 1948.

Be a Pen Pal

Imagine that you have a pen pal who lives in Beersheva. List two questions you might want to ask about the city.

1. _____

2. _____

What two things would you like to tell your pen pal about your city?

1. _____

2. _____

Kibbutzim

A kibbutz is a community where people work and live together. They share many jobs, such as planting crops and cooking meals, and rewards, such as celebrating holidays and weddings. Some kibbutzim (that's plural for kibbutz) grow fruits, such as oranges, pears, and grapes, and raise fish or other animals. Other kibbutzim manufacture computer equipment or run hotels, restaurants, or amusement parks. Kibbutz Yotvata in the Negev has a dairy that makes delicious chocolate milk!

If you lived on a kibbutz, where do you think you would want to work—in a fruit orchard? a dairy? a school? an amusement park? Why?

_____

_____

_____

Kibbutz Deganyah is located in northern Israel near Lake Kinneret. It was built in 1910 and was the first kibbutz.

On kibbutz, children go to school and help with the chores.

Daniel turned around. "Salaam!" said the man in charge of camel rides. "That's Arabic for 'shalom.'"

"Salaam!" said Daniel and Rivkah.

"Remember, it gets really hot here. It can reach 120 degrees," said Rivkah. "We've got to wear our hats, drink lots and lots of water, and— whoa! I think I found it!" called Rivkah. "I found the scavenger hunt object!"

The Negev Packing List

Draw a line between those things you will need in the Negev and the suitcase.

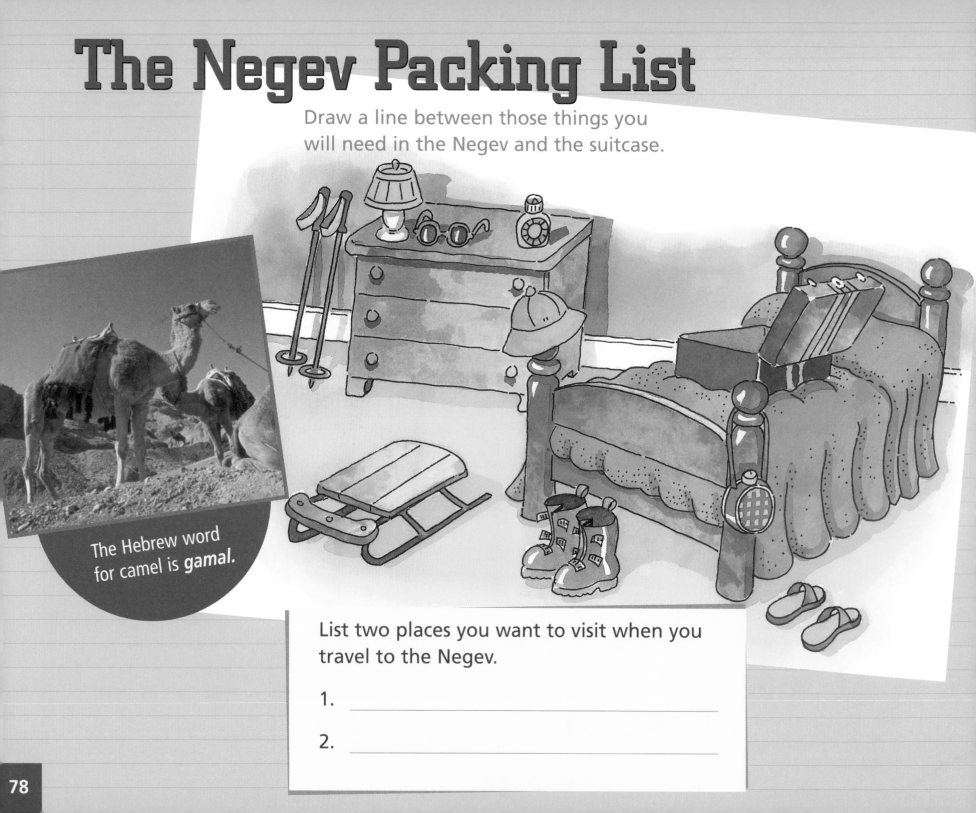

The Hebrew word for camel is *gamal*.

List two places you want to visit when you travel to the Negev.

1. _____

2. _____

Archeologists study A N ___ ___ E ___ T objects from long ago.

You can take a mud ___ ___ T H on the beach of the Dead Sea.

In ancient times, there was a fortress on top of ___ ___ ___ A D A.

Beersheva is the largest city in the N ___ ___ ___ V.

The Dead Sea's Hebrew name is Yam H ___ ___ E ___ A Ḥ, the Sea of Salt.

The password is ___ ___ ___ ___ ___, a reminder of Israel's deserts.

➤ **When your teacher says it's okay, turn to the map of Israel on pages 14–15 and place your Negev sticker in its spot!**

Eilat is a busy port and a great place to vacation.

CHAPTER 7

Eilat

Eilat

Snorkeling in the Red Sea

"*Shabbat shalom!*" people called to one another as they hurried through the streets. It was Friday afternoon. Shabbat was on its way. Stores were closing, and buses were making their last stops, but there was still so much to do! Daniel, Rivkah, and Aunt Yael finished their last-minute shopping: fresh ḥallah, a bouquet of red roses, and some cat food for Rivkah's pet, Latke—she

Many of the foods in Israeli supermarkets are just like the ones you buy at home—but their names are written in Hebrew. Can you figure out what these different foods are?

was a Ḥanukkah gift! Then they returned home to wash up, change clothes, and welcome Shabbat.

For Daniel and his family, this Shabbat would be extra special. Rivkah's friend Sarah had invited them to her house for Friday night dinner. During the walk to Sarah's house, several strangers had smiled and wished Daniel and his family a *Shabbat shalom*. At Sarah's, the glow of the Shabbat candles and the smell of the freshly baked ḥallah made Daniel feel right at home. As he picked up his napkin to place it on his lap, another clue fell out.

CLUE #6

I'm a tree that grows where it's usually hot. That's why I'm found all over Eilat!

You're the Artist!

Design an Israeli postage stamp that honors Shabbat. Before beginning, think about what you want to include on your stamp — a picture of ḥallah? candles? a family reciting Kiddush?

At the top of the stamp is the Hebrew word for Israel, *Yisrael*. At the bottom is the Hebrew word for Shabbat.

ישראל

שבת

ISRAEL

Fun Fact

Instead of dollars, Israel uses shekels. Just as there are one hundred cents in one dollar, there are one hundred agorot in one shekel.

The next day Daniel and Rivkah went to the beach with their families. The sun's rays shone on the Red Sea like a million blue crystals. Dolphins leaped from the water, and an eagle flew overhead. Everywhere he looked, Daniel saw people having fun—windsurfing, speed-boating, swimming, sailing, or just relaxing on the beach.

"Eilat is Israel's favorite vacation spot," said Rivkah. "It's sunny all year here. You can even go swimming in the winter!"

You will see the many different kinds of fish and plants that live in the sea when you visit the Underwater Observatory.

Travel below the Red Sea on the Yellow Submarine.

A Lot in Eilat!

Below is a board game that includes many of the sights found in Eilat. To travel, flip a coin. If it lands on "heads," move forward one space; if "tails," move two spaces. See who can make it to the Underwater Observatory first!

Start

North Beach
What's the hurry? Take a dip but lose a turn.

Glass-Bottom Boat
Watching the colorful fish through the bottom of the boat is so cool, you don't mind missing a turn.

Underwater Observatory
You made it!

Dolphin Reef
Swim with the dolphins and move forward one space.

Eilat Mall
Stop off for some lemonade. Use the extra energy to take another turn.

Red Sea Sports Club
Go flying into the air in a parasail and jump backward one space.

When you come to Eilat, you can swim with the dolphins!

"Ow!" said Daniel. A tiny rubber ball bounced off his head and into Rivkah's hand.

"A beach tennis ball!" said Rivkah, tossing it back to the kids who were playing beach tennis—*matkot*—one of Israel's favorite sports.

"Why don't you come play?" called one of the kids in Hebrew.

Sports Crazy!

Israel is sports *crazy*! There's soccer, basketball, tennis, volleyball—you name it! There's always a game to watch or to join in.

Here are a few fun sports facts:

There's an ice-skating rink in the Negev's largest city—Beersheva!

Every four years, athletes from around the world compete in Israel's Maccabi Games — the "Jewish Olympics"!

In 1992, Yael Arad won Israel's first Olympic medal—a silver medal in judo!

Imagine that you have been invited to take part in Israel's Maccabi Games. In what sport would you like to compete?

_____

After the Maccabi Games, which Israeli city would you like to visit first? Why?

_____

"It's more fun to use the paddle than my head," said Daniel, swatting the ball so hard that it soared through the branches of a palm tree. "Oops—sorry!" he called as he ran after it.

"That's okay," said Rivkah. "I think you found our scavenger hunt object!"

Dates grow on palm trees.

Israel uses ___ ___ E ___ E ___ S instead of dollars.

The weather is warm and S ___ ___ N ___ year round in Eilat.

You can swim with the D ___ ___ P H I ___ ___ in the Red Sea!

The Israeli M ___ C C ___ ___ I Games are held every four years.

___ E ___ ___ S ___ E ___ ___ has an ice skating rink.

The password is ___ ___ ___ ___ ___, the leaf of a palm tree. It's what we shake on Sukkot, and it's also a reminder of the palm trees that line the beaches of Eilat.

➤ **When your teacher says it's okay, turn to the map of Israel on pages 14–15 and place your Eilat sticker in its spot!**

Daniel and Rivkah packed up their beach gear.
"We've almost completed the scavenger hunt,"
said Daniel. "One more to go!"

צאתכם
לשלום

This sign wishes people peace along their way.

CHAPTER 8

Israel
LOCATOR

Home

Home

"We never found the last clue," said Rivkah as Daniel and his parents were saying their good-byes. But it was time to board the plane. Daniel and Rivkah promised that they would remain friends forever.

Loving Israel

אַהֲבַת צִיּוֹן

Israel is the homeland of the Jewish people. It is where our ancestors, including Abraham and Sarah, King David, and the prophets Deborah and Isaiah, lived. It is the land promised to the Jewish people. The mitzvah of *ahavat Tzion*—loving Israel—teaches that we should support Israel with our words and our actions. For example, we can do this by visiting and planting trees.

List two things you love about Israel.

1._____

_____

2._____

_____

List two ways you can show your love of Israel.

1._____

_____

2._____

_____

The plane disappeared into the clouds. Daniel remembered his mom saying that going to Israel would be "like coming home again." Now he understood why. Israel is where Jews everywhere are welcome and can live in freedom. It is the most holy place in the world for Jews.

A week later, Daniel lay on his bed looking at the photo album from his trip. He missed Israel, and he wondered when his next visit would be.

Suddenly he sat up. Stuck into one of the album pages was a note. The final clue!

CLUE #7

From Eilat to the Golan I fly proud and free. When you visit Israel, you're sure to find me!

He had to send Rivkah an e-mail—quickly!

At the center of the Israeli flag is a Star of David, sometimes called a Jewish star. In Hebrew, it is called *Magen David*— the Shield of David.

93

The idea for the Israeli flag was based on the tallit, the prayer shawl that Jews wear.

Dear Rivkah,

I found the last scavenger hunt piece! It's in the photos we took. The clue says: "From Eilat to the Golan I fly proud and free. When you visit Israel, you're sure to find me!" It's the Israeli flag!

Israel's national anthem is "H A ___ ___ ___ V A H", "The Hope."

The Torah teaches us that God promised Israel to ___ B R ___ H ___ M.

Ahavat Tzion is the mitzvah of ___ ___ V ___ N G Israel.

The colors of Israel's flag are B ___ ___ ___ and white.

Eretz Yisrael means the Land of ___ ___ R ___ ___ ___.

True or false: You will always be welcome in Israel: ___ R U E!

The password is ___ ___ ___ ___ ___ ___, a reminder of the Israeli flag.

➡ **When your teacher says it's okay, turn to the map of Israel on pages 14–15 and place your final sticker in its spot!**

Many Years Later...

"*My* grandfather gave this to me when *I* first went to Israel," said Daniel to his granddaughter as she got ready to board the plane. "And now," he said with a wink, "I give it to you."

ISRAEL
Certificate *of* Achievement

On this day of _____, let it be known throughout the land

DATE

that _____ has successfully completed

NAME

The Great Israel Scavenger Hunt. May _____

NAME

live a life filled with love of Torah and Israel, *ahavat Tziyon;* and may

there be peace in *Eretz Yisrael* and throughout the world.

_____
(Official Signature)

_____
(Name of School)

CERTIFICATE OF
ISRAEL
ACHIEVEMENT